Gallery Books
Editor: Peter Fallon

THE SEA WITH NO SHIPS

Frank McGuinness

THE SEA
WITH
NO SHIPS

U.S. Distributor
Dufour Editions
Chester Springs
PA 19425-0007
(610) 458-5005

Gallery Books

The Sea with No Ships
is first published
simultaneously in paperback
and in a clothbound edition
on 6 October 1999.

The Gallery Press
Loughcrew
Oldcastle
County Meath
Ireland

*All rights reserved. For permission
to reprint or broadcast these poems
write to The Gallery Press.*

© Frank McGuinness 1999

ISBN 1 85235 251 5 (*paperback*)
      1 85235 252 3 (*clothbound*)

The Gallery Press acknowledges the financial assistance
of An Chomhairle Ealaíon / The Arts Council, Ireland,
and the Arts Council of Northern Ireland.

Contents

PART ONE
Rosa O'Doherty
  Rosa O'Doherty *page* 13
  Belgium 16
  Bathe 17
  My Lover's Heart Compared to the Golden Gate Bridge 18
  The Diary of Jane Campbell 19
  St Helena 20
  Meeting at Heathrow 21
  Catacombs 22
  Southampton 23
  Mackerel Fishing off the Coast of Maine 24
  Sea-Monsters 25
  Goddess 26
  Vienna 28
  Double Dutch 29
  Valentine 32
  Roast Beef Sandwiches 33

PART TWO
A Woman Untouched
  Solomon 37
  Mrs McDermottroe 39
  A Woman Untouched 42
  Our Celibate Fathers 45
  Lavender 46

PART THREE
Van Gogh in Donegal
  The Ballina Fox 51
  Orchids in Scotland 54
  H_2O 55
  Our Lady of Kylemore Abbey 56
  Phaedra 57
  Learning in Russian 58

The Fifth Wall 59
Soul Music 60
The Red Horse 63
Killiney 64
The White Lilies 65
Innocent X 66
Trees in Spain 67
Van Gogh in Donegal 69
The Etruscan Vase 73

for Philip Tilling

PART ONE

Rosa O'Doherty

Rosa O'Doherty

d. 1660 Louvain

for Donal Gordon

I lie in Louvain, waiting for the resurrection,
A wife to a Wild Goose, a bird without wings,
Flying away from my dreams far from home.
My song is Limerick's Lament. Don't heed when I whinge.
I hear they now call it Stab City. My son
Was killed in a knife fight near here. I see the polish
Of hard steel. A stain on the floor, that's the sum
Of his life. Do you know what is my dearest wish?
To go home to Ireland and to have less patience,
To stop suffering fools. Rosa O'Doherty,
Remember my name should you forget we danced
In the graveyard of Louvain. I am ready
To forgive and fly by night since the day we sailed
To the Holy Roman empire. It lies beyond the Pale.

You should have seen the state of me upping out
Of Rathmullan. There's Donegal, my foreign fort,
Passing away from me. In my quiet way I shout,
I do not want to go. But silence is the heart's
Language. Silence is the speech of sore truth.
That I believed till the air stung my crying cheeks.
Exiles' tears are useless. Their eyes are a rath
To defend the mouth and brain from betraying ache.
I was reared a lady, virtuous, well-born.
That's what's carved on my flat tombstone. I've kept
My manners and stayed under it. Angels blow their horns
Above me, stained-glass Nativity, but women wept
In Jerusalem for the same man's lonely death.
I never shed a tear any Good Friday. Too many wreaths.

I have no time, no sympathy for my own self,
I ceased long ago to have truck with mysteries.
I have time for the wine glass, the dirty delft,
The annals of meals eaten. I have time for history
That tells me a man caught a fish, the fish spoke —
It was a wonder. Somewhere near Carndonagh,
That's where this happened. The fish was a hake.
It could tell fortunes, it could read palms, it saw
The future. The future itself looked like a dead son,
Like the sea with no ships. In Rome my husband died.
His corpse smelt of herring, fresh herring. The moon
And myself went wild. I'd hold him in my wide
Arms, hearing waves sing, You're leaving Inishowen,
Rosa O'Doherty, you'll never again see home.

Is it good to sit in the city of Louvain
Drinking water? That's all I can manage,
Remembering Ireland, remembering the pain.
My stomach is churning, this water tastes foreign.
My hands have turned into cats' claws, they have the itch
To kill. I could catch a rat with my teeth.
It would taste like raspberry jam, sweet — still each
To her own. But when it's devoured, my breath
Would be sour as a widowed man dreaming
Of his dead wife. Of his own holy family.
Mine was never holy. It's just that we took wing
As Wild Geese never to return. I'd lost the keys
To my kingdom. Neither nuns nor priests honour us.
Before I noticed, we had turned into dust.

I'm blessed with an excellent constitution.
I can guzzle whatever's put in front of me.
Shellfish, lamb, the daintiest pastry — all one
In the sight of God, who did not create the sea
Nor the mountain where the lamb thrived, nor
The fish that sing to me from the generous plate,
Their bones a sacred relic. It is far
From shell and mountain I now reside. The flat
Lands of resignation, in Flanders I abide.
My land-locked city, my Louvain, my grave —
If I squealed like a pig leaving Ireland, I hid
It all. I had to. I was the chieftain's wife.
How do I look to this alien people? Red,
Encased in passion flower, I neither smiled nor bled.

But Jesus, I long for the sleep of the just.
My eyes have not closed in this country.
In my dreams I'm not myself. I do as I must.
Were an angel to appear, my brother, sister,
I would burst my banks and roar out my name.
I am Rosa O'Doherty, on this earth born to wander,
Born near the River Crana, a woman now at home
To every dog and devil who kneels before her,
Now that she is lying in a grave in Louvain.
I sometimes wonder about going to America.
I wonder if we go home, will we be fleeced?
That's another story, another saga.
I'd love eight hours sleep and wake up at peace.

Belgium

Without you in Belgium,
The chocolate's bitter.
I never touch chocolate.

Without you in Belgium,
The mussels lack salt.
The shell deserts the sea.

Without you in Belgium,
I cannot speak Flemish
And make no fist of it.

Without you in Belgium,
It rains, and the weather
Is what you make of it.

Without you in Belgium,
The gorgeous chairs in
Horta's Museum are empty.

Without you in Belgium,
Rick's American Café
Doesn't serve pale Margaritas.

Without you in Belgium,
La Grande Place is abandoned,
There's no hurdy-gurdy.

Without you in Belgium,
My hair is too long.
I'll cut it, I'll comb it.

Bathe

My love bathes in
The wet of my eyes.
He dries under
The sun of himself.

No need for rain,
He has my eyes.
No need for night,
I sleep with the sun.

My Lover's Heart Compared to the Golden Gate Bridge

For a start it is not golden
Nor is it a bridge.
      It is an animal,
It is mineral, and the question is,
Does it love itself? It does,
But with discretion.
      I adore discretion,
For the heart is capable of being ripped
Apart, repaired as if nothing happened,
Repainted, but not golden.
        It is red,
The heart.

The Diary of Jane Campbell

after Ammi Phillips, itinerant painter of portraits, San Diego

My mother and I stitch calico
For curtains. My grandmother too.
These save our house from the sun.
My mother's name is Sarah,
I am seven, I cradle a doll.
It looks like me and my mother.
My body's a frock, red as Mama's face.
The painter who saw me saw that.

Calico, embroidered with lace,
My mother touches — how delicate.
I love her. Mama is delicate.
She may well die in childbirth, but
I will cover this continent seeking
Her; transformed by an itinerant painter,
My geometry America, my compass myself.
This is the diary of Jane Campbell.

I count the pieces of my life
In the brown crystal ball of
My country. I'll marry for life
And have seven children, all with my eyes.
The hunter who trapped me forever,
That painter, had eyes, eyes like a
Needle stitching calico for a shroud,
But not mine. Not Jane Campbell.

St Helena

This day we drive by way of Muir Woods
And, scented by the holy redwoods,
We do not find the true cross in the
Calvary of vineyards, the brown mountains
Of St Helena. There, safely inland,
I remember the ocean, the Pacific
Goddess, where stands the rock filled
With brown pelicans. Had I a Saviour,
It would be that bird stabbed in the mouth,
Now held in sanctuary. Feeding it fish,
I'd worship its hunger, powerless
And screeching, deeply ungrateful.

Meeting at Heathrow

They've made it user friendly, the airport.
You smoke in designated areas.
Now the war's come to an end, security
Is strict but beards are not suspicious.
I long to see you before we check in.
British Airways to Rome. Flight from Dublin,
Trek the long mile, cursing heavy luggage.
You're there, snatching a quick fag. Coffee shop.
You all over. I take sight of you, happy man
To see me. For you I've brought my passport,
I've not missed the plane, I have the tickets
Safe. Thank God. You're an atheist, but not
A good one. When the plane takes off, you pray.
I'll tell on you. I always do. Trust me.
I'm tempted to compare you to planes, birds,
But you take flight in ways more mysterious.
Speak Italian, I won't understand you.
You make me happy in Heathrow Airport.
I'm with you, and glad you know the language.

Catacombs

They are always plural, the catacombs,
As if one did not die alone.

How comforting. Do you remember us
Visiting them, that crying child?

Do you remember his name? Years ago.
He'd nearly be a grown man now.

Was he spoilt, ruined beyond repair?
There are reasons for not believing so.

To condemn a child for crying,
That's not fair. Not fair —

That fight in Rome, those words I cried.
Not fair, you're not fair.

But you are a just man.
I love you for many reasons. Justice

Is one of them. I'm not just,
Should you judge me with severity.

I went into the bathroom, washed
My face, kissed you in water. The kiss

Of remembering the last time in Rome,
The catacombs, the crying child.

Do you remember, through tears,
His name? It was Douglas.

He was frightened of the dark,
Of dying alone. So am I.

Southampton

I should not be singing this unending song.

I should have gone to Southampton and rescued
Myself from a boy whom Belfast beat into silence.
There is no silence more sincere than the break of a heart

That may have stopped breaking because I didn't know the clues.
When I look at our lives, I know we didn't want to part,
But we did, and that's an end to it, I tell myself.

Still, my heart's stronger than I am, a strange dance
Of blood and brain. Let them dance, it was our wish,
But my heart could do with a cleaning, a Protestant polish.

Not that he was a Protestant, this boy whose eyes were blue
As the veil I drew discretely over my patent shoes.
I trod on him, he trod on me, then my mother got involved —

Involved in a war of betrayal, he betrayed me young.
Why? Leave it at that as a riddle to be solved.
I touch his face like a cup of cracked china delft.

Yet riddle me this: Say I had gone to Southampton
And said, I am wasting my youth in the red light district
Of this town, would he have given me a son?

I should not be singing this unending song.

Mackerel Fishing off the Coast of Maine

for Ira and Phyllis Wender

They should catch mackerel off the coast of Maine
But they don't.
It's a shame.
The sea there is crying out for able-bodied men —

Men who see the point
Of fishing so many thousand miles from base
And see the silver of these fish like delicate lace,
Carrickmacross lace, in the pillows

Of the surf of the waves of the Atlantic Ocean.
They would sleep in the sea,
Were they unlucky.
The water would taste like gin distilled from sloes,

Sloes picked from the bushes whose leaves
Were butter and cheese.
What is butter, what is cheese to a man
Fishing for mackerel off the coast of Maine?

I would leave that answer to the fortunate, free mackerel.
They say, We will lead them to hell,
We who are ocean and salt and bone,
We who know hell off the coast of Maine is far from home.

Sea-Monsters

I believe in sea-monsters.
I say, Peace be to you, dear monsters.
In the name of God trouble us no more.

Neither He nor they listen.
Boats are dragged down, and statues of the Virgin
That blessed the sea, crack.

Sailors cling to miraculous medals as if they were rafts,
But cheap silver dissolves.
Men asleep were nearly naked,

All they wore was the unfortunate medal
Of silver flesh and golden chain.
The chain breaks.

It wasn't golden, not the chalice
Of blood and bread, but wine
And water, salt water.

The sea-monster's eyes were deranged with salt tears.
So they ate the boats.
They were hungry for human flesh.

That's what they desire. Then they grieve,
Though they've satisfied themselves.
They say, Let's do this again soon.

They do. But they're superstitious.
They count their dead in phone numbers
And rely on the sea for information.

It says, Peace be to you, good monsters,
In the name of God trouble us no more.
Yet we do, and they dine.

Goddess

When you fall in love with a Greek god
It is not wise to give him a ring.
In case Pallas Athena should answer,
And that bitch would turn you into an owl,
An old woman who knows too much
About falling in love. Then he leaves,
The Greek god, plays Poseidon, to raise
The sinking ship of your life and save
You from the jetsam of love, as if love
Were a language derived from the Greek.

I meet my queer friend in Heathrow,
And he's got gold for wine and vodka,
Throw in a coffee to keep me sober,
And I'll spill all over the place,
This bloody cavern before the flight —
The flight to where — not fucking Egypt —
I'm no Virgin, sick with a child,
For I love my tender babies, God
Forgive me, I'm possessed by love,
By sorrow, I'm turning into a prophetess.

I could tell you all about Poseidon.
He loves lips that could suck the sea,
I am an icon of the ocean kissed
By sailors, safe to sail in. So they think.
They do not know my squalls, my rage.
I myself could cause disaster, but
I won't. That's not my climate. My lips
Have power of feeling. I kiss my friends,
They kiss me. What's a kiss? The Greek god
Told me I have powers to raise the sun.

When I miss my absent Poseidon, I play
A game he played on me. I tell myself
The sea is suffering, though I know
It not to be. That's when I embroider
Fiction with the fact I am not alone.
This gives me strength and consolation.
I could tear a temple down about my eyes,
My legs, my heart; I gave my heart for
The taking and he took — well, mercy me.
A woman not forgiving. But, forgive me.

Vienna

Sweet love,
I'd serve you in Vienna
To the poor and to the gentry.

Serve you,
And let you fight your corner
As you would and as you could.

Train me,
Like a splendid white horse
To command,

To man in time,
To whisper.
Sweet love, eat.

Double Dutch

for Lucas

1 THE BRIDGE AT KILLINEY BEACH

When Jesus breathed on sand the words to condemn the woman
Taken in adultery, what did he carve that so scared the men
About to stone her?
                    Could it be, You have known her?
My Jesuit uncle, whom I loved as a child, his answer
Would be different. I visited him in America, as did all
My brothers. In its way America was too beautiful,
Too big, too lonely, unlike the close and sorrowful land
Of the Low Countries that I need so much. Hand
On heart, I cling to my country tightly, for sorrow,
That's my mother dying when I was twenty. Still raw,
That wound, do not notice it, please. You have, I talk
Too much, yes, but I'm not unaware, I watch like a hawk
As well. I'm Dutch, and Catholic, confession is enough
To spill the beans.
               Enough. Shaw left money in his will
To reform the English language, the way they spell
Is erratic, and if my memory serves me, *enough*
He used as an example to prove how strange and hard
Is orthography — is that the correct word?
My words to you standing on a bridge at this beach,
The two of us watching swallows pattern the wish
For flight into means of saying something,
The two of us content to be here standing,
To be flying into a heaven of friendship
That is strictly on this earth, I let slip
That my father studies the creatures of the air,
And he read cookbooks surviving the Winter of Hunger.
The War. No bread, no tomatoes, no potatoes, no birds.

2 BALLAD OF THE HANGING MAN

after François Villon

Were my brothers, my compass corners, to see me
Hanging by the straggy neck of Ben Bulben Mountain,
Would they be all ears learning from my last will and
   testament?
Like heaven they would, the same, they'd *baa* like lost sheep
And pray that we should all avoid the slaughter-house.
Pray Christ it is not Easter all the long year round.
The moon could then turn into a malevolent sister
And she would try to fix the date for every marriage.
The flesh I know so well would collapse into bed
And I could sleep alone like the sun at night. Forgive —

That's what it all comes down to. The mistakes I've made,
The mistakes I will make, so what? I've laughed and bad
Judgements might acquit themselves, passing into signs of
   love
Long gone. No one on Ben Bulben Mountain could listen
To my earnest pleading, so selfish, I recollect the days
And sons I've lived my lost life through. Drunken
Telephone calls, yes, I regret them, the flex of the phone
A noose, sufficient rope to hang myself. I did them.
I spoke in a way that shocked me. I was desperate,
I was out of it. I was nineteen again, virginal. Forgive —

That's what it all comes down to. I caught sight on
Ben Bulben Mountain of magpies and crows. Birds of bad
Omen, but not to me, for they were good companions
To a solitary man wandering the hot west of Ireland.
I could bear its siroccos, they were like whispers,
Saying to me, We can blow you hither and thither,
You are at our mercy, but you don't believe in mercy,

So we will lift you in your light heart and lead
You safely down the mountain and you will understand
The reasoning behind wind and water. Forgive —

That's what it all comes down to. If hell is like
Ben Bulben Mountain, then I can face it, Archangel,
I can climb into its flames and not squeal.
Heaven will be like Venice when I was nineteen,
Hanging by my fingernails to a man I loved.
Forgive him. Forgive myself. That's what it comes to.

Valentine

I gave my love my life to wear.
He braided it into his hair.
And with a comb of honey steel,
I tasted him, I touched his skin.
But life is fleeting as the wind,
Sweet love rotates, a turning wheel.
Above his grave, carve this headstone —
My love has left, he lies alone.

Roast Beef Sandwiches

Is that my father, driving in the van,
The Gothic lettering spelling out his name,
Patrick McGuinness & Son?
Is he coming from the Drift Inn?
Is the van cream and blue, the spelling red?
And what shall he cast upon the sea water?

Roast beef sandwiches.
Are they in the pocket of his brown overalls,
Smelling of bread dust and broken buttons?
Will we feast this night on beef and tomatoes and onions
And bread, always bread, Father?
Roast beef sandwiches.

PART TWO

A Woman Untouched

Solomon

in memory of Máire de Paor

I have the wisdom of Solomon.
This year, the year's end,
I'll swim back, wearing the costume

Of my Bible, black swimming costume,
Flattering, to the town
Of my birth. A Moses basket,

This town will end in a river,
An Egyptian river, a delta, an omega,
But the alphabet will be trees,

For in this Egypt, by this river,
The slaves, and those served by slaves,
Will speak in something earlier than

Gaelic. I will decipher it. Them.
My river, my trees, my place of birth.
I will be able to read the waves,

The pages of the Atlantic. I'll dig
For light in the oceanic grey of
A lake of shadows. My home. For

Sentiment's sake, I could name it,
My home, my town, my river, my trees,
Buncrana, but I am not sentimental.

I was the doctor's daughter.
Excavate the street of this town, this lake,
This ocean, you'll find me nowhere.

That is why I have the sense of place,
The instinct of home, the bracelet on
The wrist identifying the lost continent

Of the truth waiting to be told.
I could not wait to escape.
The continental shift of love and desire,

I knew it, crossed it, crossed as if it were
The street, the one street, the same street
Of the Egyptian town where I was born.

That's where they found the tomb of Alexander.
It was false. Where the source of the Nile
Was not. But there were trees, graves, a river —

Some sort of wisdom. Each year, to that river,
The salmon returned. Wise as Solomon,
I am the salmon this year returning,

To the town, the lake, the river of her birth.
Spawned when the moon had a head on its shoulders,
I will dig for gold. The gold of shadows.

Who knows what I will find in these fields?
Buncrana? I was the doctor's daughter.
My home, my town, my river, my trees.

Mrs McDermottroe

for Maria and Conor

If that eejit, Carolan, decides to welcome me
To the angelic orders — I'm not more suited for heaven
Than I am for Dublin, and if God's own holy kingdom
Remotely resembles that kip of West Brits, I'm out of it —
But if the angels, by any chance, are harping on Carolan's
Concerto — which, by the by, is not a concerto in the right
Sense of the word, and you should know that, you have a
 degree,
Money wasted, money down the drain, I blame myself,
I let you go to Dublin; Galway, now that's a town,
But you would not listen to me, well and good, may
You stew in it, where was I? I remember, Carolan,
I'll have the manners to listen to his harping.

Oh go on. Laugh. Have a good laugh at your mother.
You've been doing it since you leapt, my first born,
My love, my beautiful daughter, my own girl —
Why am I talking like this? Have you slipped
Whiskey into this coffee? I would not put it past you —
Jesus, I've done it to myself when I wasn't looking —
Since you leapt laughing from my womb, you were always
The one I could never predict. Other children cried
To face the world, but not the lady with the lamp here,
She was out charming the doctor and the nurses
In the hospital, into the way of the world, trained
To know it by instinct, by herself. Herself alone.

Look at her — out like a June robin in November.
Christ knows the way this generation's going,
But the man with her, leading her astray —
Not that the devil himself could lead that one astray —

Whatever he calls himself, he's still Donegal,
And, as a decent Sligo woman, I know about Donegal
And all their doings — may God forgive them,
They broke Fianna Fáil's heart, they did, but I
Forgive them. The North's broke many a heart.
I look some days from the window of my house,
I see Lough Gill. I could weep tears to fill it
Over again — I should not watch the evening news.

I should rely for information on the post office,
People tell you everything if you're behind a counter,
And I swear to God and His blessèd mother
I have not repeated a word of what would harm
Any human being, well versed as I am in the sorrow
And stupidity of what hurts the innocent.
Whatever else you may throw against me, don't
Throw that I'm a cruel woman, because I'm not.
Life might have made me weary of easy words,
All promises can be broken, the best can be the worst,
But I've never lost faith in — never lost faith —
What would be the point of living without faith?

I must tell you a story, in case I forget it,
So that you will remember it off by heart.
One evening on the train from sweet Sligo,
The town that same evening like a girl from
Years ago, getting married to the man she loved,
Shy and kind but not showing it — him, the man;
And her, like the town that summer's day, soft,
Lonely although it was jammed with strangers,
And she was a stranger to him, the bride, the groom —
Where was I? I remember, the train, me sleeping,
And the story is that I forgot where I was going,
I could not for the life of me remember —

So, didn't I turn to the person sleeping beside me,
I nudged her shoulder and I asked civilly,
Do you by any chance know if this train is going to
Sligo? Didn't the whole train grind to a halt?
Was there sheep on the line? I asked myself.
I looked out the train window, there was Lough Gill.
I looked at the sleeping woman. It was my daughter.
And I was happy. A happy woman, dreaming.
The train started up, I was on my way home.
So stop this crying, my sleeping child.
It's all right, I'm home now, it is all right.
It could be worse, daughter. It could be Donegal.

A Woman Untouched

for Anne O'Callaghan

    1

I am flying to California on Virgin Airlines
When the death of Helen is announced in Ireland.

Let the sky turn metallic and weep buckets.
Let my hands be raised in supplication.

It cannot be so. Most beautiful Helen,
I am not prepared for her eternity.

She is the loveliest, the most gentle of women,
She the funniest, the best of all times.

Helen is dead. Let the heavens rip open
The veil of the temple of the sweet Atlantic.

Is that her soul ascending? Helen,
There is laughter in the whole happiness

Of your friendship. For your thirty-three years
You have graced this earth. Grace the air I fly.

Give me strength through grace to say savage words.
Helen is dead. Helen of Troy is dead.

2

She moved through life like a woman untouched.
Her honest face concealed its secrets.
When she chose to speak, there was wisdom stirring.
She kept her counsel, she believed in fate.

Believing in wisdom, she faced it squarely.
Poor fate didn't know what it had taken on.
All fights, my friend, are fights to the bitter end.
As soon stop the sun shining as the end be sweet.

3

You say I was beautiful — and I was.
Yet beauty is a mask of beaten gold.
I might approve of this appellation,
This Helen of Troy, were it ever true.
But it's not. So, call me by my own name.
Say it, even if it breaks your heart.
Do you not think my heart is broken?
Do you think mythology eases my pained heart?
One day I looked at myself in a mirror.
The loveliest woman in Ireland looked out at me.
I told her where to get off that instant.
I'm a working woman. I've a job to do.
That woman in the mirror then laughed like myself.
My strength is that I can see through myself.

4

The spring is coming to California.
In Booterstown Avenue a palm tree grows.

Exotic growth, no place to be here,
Like yourself, Anne O'Callaghan.

No chance now it will be ever uprooted
From shading my house. Dance on its leaves

And let your soul ascend as a tree ascends.
I phone Kaye Fanning from California.

She said, She's dead, our loved girl is dead.
I cried for an hour in a motel room.

Early morning there, late night at home.
I went out and taught Anton Chekhov. *Three Sisters*.

I call on the sister of the spring that comes
To California, of the palm tree that grows

In Booterstown Avenue, flying on Virgin Airlines.
The sky turned metallic and weeping buckets.

She the loveliest, the most gentle of women,
She the funniest, the best of all times.

Helen is dead. Let the heavens rip open
The veil of the temple of the sweet Atlantic.

Our Celibate Fathers

Our celibate fathers sleep alone, in separate rooms.
Long ago they upped and left their devoted wives.
I put it all down to an itch, an incurable itch,
The scratch in the innocent loins of young men,
That made them want to father in the very first place.
I blame the purple of their uncontrollable desire,
For purple is a notoriously difficult colour to paint,
And they were smitten by that lack of celibacy,
The need to reproduce themselves as saints.
Saints they were, our celibate fathers, saints they would be.
Their children went to Limbo. They were born dead,
They were baptised, and they grew into men and women,
Healthy to all intents and purposes, except in one respect.
This respect was that they sided with the mother.
This caused bother. Big bother. The family divided,
The holy family that gathered for feast days, holy days,
Days of obligation, fast days, funerals, days of birth,
Of marriage, when the whole rigmarole started off again.
A feed of sprouts from Brussels, ham and turkey,
Two types of spuds, roast and mashed, this was served
On a tablecloth white as an altarboy's soutane.
Then someone would remember who dropped the good book,
Let it clatter through the agony of the kitchen,
Pages through the garden, where a single dahlia grew,
Whose petals were scarlet. Strip the dahlia bare,
You'll find a fist. She went mad, the mother rejected.
I date it from there, the end of the marriage.
The pope had blessed the union of our celibate parents,
His hawk face waiting for the night when he came out and
Hunted for their desires. He found them, he married them.
And the bed they once shared overlooked the football field.
It was green and fair, it was Ireland. Itch and scratch.

Lavender

for Theresa

They harvest lavender in Norfolk.
Nights I have spent with you, Tristram,
Packing innocent lavender into sachets,
Your fingers the perfume of Arabia.
When I think of you, it's lavender,
Packed for profit. Money, my dear,
Does not grow on trees. We know that,
But don't believe it. The day you died —
Spare me from the day you died. My dear,
A lilac bush in Booterstown, famine flower,
Should not be brought into the house,
As if you were famine, as if you were dead,
As if my house were anywhere but where
You are welcome, you, my harvest,
My Arabia, my night, my sorrow —
No sorrow for you, my dear.
Let me show you the kingdoms of the earth.
All this is yours, if you marry me.
Marry someone else. Someone wonderful.
Have children. Children like lavender.
There are nights I cry to your soul.
Your soul is always sensible.
Purgatory, my dear, skip it.
I wait for you in Paradise.
They harvest lavender in Paradise.
It is not remotely like Norfolk.

PART THREE

Van Gogh in Donegal

The Ballina Fox

for Dorothea

I eat what food is mine.
I'm blonde. I'm unique.
My hair is wonderful *poitín*.
I am the Ballina fox.

I've my own way. I watch
The hounds. I steer clear
Of the pack. I'm handsome.
I don't expect thanks.

Not a word in my language.
Language is like the moon.
The moon is sweet cheese.
I don't eat cheese.

I would not thank you for it,
But I'd thank you for friends.
So they howl at the moon.
I trust those who howl.

They, like myself, have partaken
Of heather, gorse, pros and cons
Of love. Don't cod me
With affection. I eat love.

I believe in it, but
No humankind will win
This one. I know my landscape,
It charms me, the landscape

Of Ballina, and I,
Lock, stock and barrel,
Upped and outed. Chased,
Turning into a hound,

I asked it for forgiveness.
God forgives those who forget
Themselves. Well, damn him.
I'll drink good wine.

It's lucky. Luck is with
The Ballina fox. She's vixen.
She runs wild.
A woman running wild.

She'll be happy as a man.
Were I man, not fox,
I'd be less happy.
That much is true.

So much is true I've come
To hate the truth. I like
What is less, what is hungry.
If words were food

I'd dine on morsels.
I'd feed on fine language.
But I'm the Ballina fox,
I say what I mean.

I'm blonde. I'm unique.
My hair is wonderful *poitín*.
I'm fertile as gorse.
I grow like heather,

And I love my cubs.
I'm fox, I'm vixen.
Let me run wild like
Jesus. I'm the Ballina fox.

Orchids in Scotland

for Evelyn and Sam

They are wild men, these pink orchids,
Light as silver, light as pints are heavy.
They bear their weight full of grace
As the orchid bears its sense of
Adoration on a Japanese altar,
Arranged to wrestle with the gods.
My money is on the silver orchids.

H_2O

for Dorothy MacGabhann

I taste of God, and he does not exist.
My favourite drink is iced water.
Not this concoction of alcohols.
I am the gift of God. Some nights I exist
Only in the remembered stain of water,
The River Jordan. I stand a round of
What I remember. It is my childhood.
An aunt, in Middlesbrough, clutching
Her breasts to herself as if a woman
Were easy to clutch as water is easy
To drink. My favourite, iced water.
My eyebrows are soft, my lashes gentle.
I am not afraid. Why should I be?
Perhaps of myself. Myself, my perhaps.

Our Lady of Kylemore Abbey

for Olwen Fouéré

I appeared out of purdah on this mountainside,
A statue overlooking the lake at Kylemore, white
And hardfaced. They called me the mother of God, as if
He needed a mother, as if I needed a God.

There are those who wonder about my present position.
A woman suspended on a pedestal. I don't like it,
But it's a living, and it beats what I used to do.
This involved melting the salt from the sea,

Writing the Bible in the salt so distilled, dipping
The parchment in fresh water and giving solace
To men who weep, to women giving birth to a mountain.
Mercy made me Our Lady of Kylemore Abbey.

From that day on, though, I lost all heart, all interest,
Receiving the worship of lonely girls, rowing in the lake,
Girls like myself once, waiting for husbands to sail
Into fertile places. They never arrived, these husbands —

They had wives at home to conquer. Yet I loved
The smell of their ships. They caught fish, I fire
And used it to burn their boats. They drowned then in the
    arms
Of other women. My husbands dead, I went into purdah

And veiled my face, Our Lady of Kylemore Abbey.
I dressed in this white and gave to the poor.
I gave them the mercy that once hardened me
When I was raw and awkward but full of grace.

Phaedra

I looked under my bed.
There was a stepladder.
I climbed it and fought
With an angel of the Lord.
I opened a can of worms
And fed them to the children
Of the father who'd left his wife
The night before they perished.

Those kids were streetwise
And wouldn't eat this filth,
So I took them out fishing
And used them for bait.

They refused to drown.
I opened my heart and
Said, I love your father.
They spoke in baby talk:

I was not their mother.
The children of the father
Who once upon a time left his wife
To court another. She's doing

Pretty well, that first wife,
Making money hand over fist,
So they say. Some nights she remembers
Their father and she smiles.

She says, I know what he likes.

Learning in Russian

for Stephen Rea

I have a niece who prays for love, convinced
In the end God will speak and save this place,
Should it be worth the salt of salvation.
Do I believe this? What have I to lose?
This is all I own. A run-down estate,
That abacus, my fingers and my thumbs,
And the knowledge my labour was thankless.
Sore labour it was. Sore sorrow it brought.
Still they cling to the estate, fingers, thumbs,
As if its fields were braille, but I'm not blind,
Nor Russian either. I am not Russian.
This I'll tell myself when the harvest's gathered.
A good harvest, but not mine. I'm let know
That. Though I've toiled in the barren office
Where fingers and thumbs, the tools of my trade,
Planted flax and potatoes, and I smell of linseed —
Forget it. No laments. What's done is done.
I'll return to the abacus. Fingers, thumbs.
The run-down estate? Still beautiful. Mine.

The Fifth Wall

for Patrick Mason

I know this place. It's been here before.
It is recognised by smells of burning,
For a fire ate it and gave it shape.
Having been on fire, it fears nothing,
Nothing, that is, but the fifth wall.
This is the wall that is visible
Only to those who have charged over it,
The wall that defies all description,
The wall that heard the pity and the terror;
It stood unmoved on its firm foundations,
But its soul was swaying and might have broken
Through the brick and clay and dust.
Should you intend to rebuild that wall,
It is first necessary to recognise it.
Strike a match against it to give light.
What will be seen? That would be telling,
And telling is the business of the fifth wall.
Telling and swaying and pity and terror.
I'll know this place. It will be again,
For a fire eats it and gives it shape.

Soul Music

for Joan Sheehy

I phoned up my soul, asked it out. Declined,
My soul. There had just been an opening night,
It was worn out. It had donned blue bow-ties —
I hate my soul when it's wearing blue —
And the ties were lost somewhere in London,
Or Dublin, or New York. I fear for it,
This soul of mine, should it enter its head
It's had enough of this strange groove and not bop
Anymore. Not cry at its party. Poor soul,
The centre of my playful earth, I'll sin
No more. I'll give away my worldly goods.
I'll start from scratch. We'll love like boys in heat.
Would you like that, dear soul?
                                    What would you know?
It says, *You who gave me to words and time?*

I did not give you to words nor time.
You gave yourself to music. Your mother
Had a fabulous voice, you were inspired
To copy her. Now look at the mess made. Wine
Stains on the walls of your body, needles
In the veins of your mother. She's red
With weeping. You did this. No excuses. Dead
Words, dead time. You're the ghost of herself.
I don't forgive you for your terrible lies.
You swore the truth to me. You gave me lies.
But what lies, you say, *what beautiful lies.*
There's no beauty in the soul's deception.
It was you deceived me, your cracked mirrors.
I looked into them. There was nothing there.

If there was nothing, then why are you here?
Why are you hell-bent on ripping my heart?

You know the heart is fragile as the mind,
Fragile as memory. Remembering you,
I must be here, but you question the nights
I laid in love, touching you.
      It's yourself
You love, the soul replies, *You cannot love*
That which is lost, and I am now lost
Forever, love.
     The soul is a smart bugger.
Do you know how much this call is costing?
Are you in Dublin, London, New York?
The soul is also a tight bugger. Cash
Counts for something in ethereal terms.
The soul laughs for the material world.

Laugh on, you bollox, see if I care.
We've had this endless fight before.
Endless, eternal, my beautiful soul.
You left me? Well, so be it, damn you.
Were you to come back, I would bar the door,
Break the windows, clear the place, get the Guards,
Have you removed. You're out of order, boy,
You are, you know.
      Then bar the door to me,
He whispers, *You don't need to, I'm not there.*
Nor will I be while you betray me. Boy,
You call me, but I'm the man who made you
Man. If you want me, say you're sorry.
No, not sorry. Tell me the whole story.
In roars and whispers, if that is your way.

There was a man who came from the sea,
Came onto land to lose his soul. He did
And danced a jig for it through Paradise,
For nothing ventured, nothing lost. The soul

Turned to the sea. He settled down and stopped
The dancing. They say his soul fished for men.
He bought a house with loads of ghosts, a house
To rear his wildest dreams. Did they come true?
Last night he saw a naked shape pick up
The phone and call — who was it? Was it the sea?
Was it his soul? They met again, face to face,
And sang a song into the ocean. It said,
Sisters, should you need me, phone someday
And I will answer.

The Red Horse

For twenty-five years I've heard this horse.
It is red, by and large. Its wooden heart
Burns when it sees a fence, yet its four feet
Jump like a young one in order to win.
Win what? Is it money or is it fame?
I don't know what it is it's trying to win
With the effort of jumping, but it's not happy,
The red horse, though it continues to ride.
It will ride itself into extinction.
It thinks extinction will bring happiness.
Why? Because the long dead must be happy
In their way of scaling the scariest jump,
Leaps that take the breath away, a horse called
Goodbye.
         When I say, by and large
It is red, this horse, it has a black saddle,
And green and yellow stirrups.
Its tail is speckled, and so's the mane.
There are no colours in dreams, so
It has ceased to believe in colours, for
It is surely a creature from dreams,
This red horse, black and green, and
Speckled colourless gold. No one rides it,
For it is in control only of itself.
Hence its propulsion forward, riddles,
Dreamless, colourless. It has ceased to be,
But it's in love with forward motion.
It is no longer coming whence it came.
Having forgotten where it was first born,
How can it win? Where's its destination?
It is trying to recover the red.
Should it succeed, it will stop leaping,
It will stop dreaming. It will be the red horse.
For twenty-five years I've heard this horse.
It is my friend, and yes, it is my dream.

Killiney

for Christine Sheridan

The daughters of the King of Leinster built this cathedral,
The marvellous daughters who did not die in childbirth
But chose instead to divert the Irish Sea to Jerusalem
And, failing that, did succeed in converting Killiney to the
  Holy Land.

These marvellous daughters, all silver and generous of spirit,
Loved their father, the King of Leinster, above the men of
  Ulster,
Connaught, Munster, although these selfsame men swore
  damnation,
Plenty, peace, harmony to the beautiful daughters.

There in Killiney, they chose to repeat themselves as if
By repetition they could bring their strange father, the king,
Back to life, they could live forever as daughters, as sisters,
To end the endless quarrel of who was loved most, loved by

The father. Since they knew only too well none was loved,
Their mother had died many years before the quarrel,
Before their father became the son of the King of Leinster,
Their angry words were music, evidence of music

That they had learned at the knee of their dead father.
My father is dead, they roared, my father dead,
And the cathedral, generous in spirit, in silver, received
The corpse of their father, the mother, the daughters of the
  king.

The White Lilies

Casablanca — my white room.
Casablanca, white lilies.
These stems fit the long vase.
Lie there, good legs in the air.
A seafaring man, their mate,
The vase, their handsome husband,
Returns from empty oceans,
Waiting to be water-filled.
It is straight and narrow,
Its houses the white lilies.
They thrive here in Borneo,
A Borneo of learning,
A mess of books, of atlas,
Defying its description,
Defying all description.
The vase is repetitious,
Its scarlet face is scarlet;
It considers lilies,
How they've spinned, toiled,
To great avail.
They make a dress for windows,
A bridal dress — they've married
Windows, doors and walls.
The lilies are bigamous,
They fall in love four times, more
So in the mirror, more, more
White lilies. White lilies,
Casablanca in my house.

Innocent X

Pope Innocent X, painted by Velasquez,
Harmonious the composition, the savagery of colour.
Hard the face that does not forgive.
Terrible the eyes that look out forever.
Blessed by the love that conceived the trinity.
He has not known such love, Pope Innocent X.
Why did Velasquez love him then, to paint with forgiveness?
Money, perhaps. Money is always perhaps.
There is money in the chimes of his clothes.
But the clothes don't fit him, he is naked,
A naked pope, celibate and lonely. Handsome is
As handsome does, and lonely is lonely.

Trees in Spain

for Brian Bourke

Remember the woman
Who put masks in the trees
Not to scare
But to speak with the birds?

Magyar and Swiss,
She was thought mad
As a brush
Carved from the branches of

Trees in Spain.
Here the lemon
And olive
Are shades of blue,

And the fireworks begin.
The mortified leaves
And halo
Of cloud are celebrating.

This is the feast day
When trees in Spain
Are worshipped.
Bark is blessed and eaten.

Rivers are black with the sun
And that goat
Is molten gold.
Everything shelters under

Trees in Spain,
For all the eye remembers
Is the mask
Of a woman speaking with birds.

And her face is the trees.

Van Gogh in Donegal

for Gerald Dawe

I caught wind of change off the Hook of Holland
And set sail for Ireland, a country of potatoes.
I could smell the blight and the skeletal faces
Grown fat on the sweetness of surviving the odds.
They may teach me a lesson about disease
But I doubt it, so that was not my intention.
No, I was searching for diamonds in the soil
Of a starved and dumb country whose language I knew
Only by gesture and colour and look,
And I would fall in love on the island of Ireland.

My puritan soul found no whores in Dublin,
The city was stinking with virginal men
Who'd cut out their tongues in protest against
The temptation of mouths. I renounced paint
And paper and colour. I swear I was blind
To the endearing young charms of girls
And their mothers. I got my comeuppance and, happy,
I headed to the very far north. A clarinet sea
Doctored to me. It said, Play away
But wash your feet nightly for, like Amsterdam,

You'll sweat like lost souls, and lost souls deliver
Nothing. I found comfort in the whisper of mermaids,
Girls with waves in their hair, hair like red horses,
But in the end they were looking for sailors
Who promised at best a love unrequited.
I became a prophet and preached well-worn sermons,
Worn as shoes that stank on my feet, and socks
Were wool and thread from New Zealand, my home
In the New World where I should have gone, but
I travelled north to Ireland, north to Donegal.

The journey was hectic, the food unspeakable,
But reason was my guide, and the stars were logic.
I was a white man in this green country,
So I slept out in the fields and thereby turned green.
Thus I could pass absolutely unnoticed,
A farmer, a tinker, a man without colour,
Yet the treacherous sun turned my skin to yellow,
And for once in my life I was Japanese.
I spoke Dutch to them and they could see Asia,
My words were like placenames from the Far East.

Monaghan, Cavan and County Tyrone
Exotic as Tokyo, Kyoto and Siam,
Places like ghosts, my unforgiving father
Bearing witness to my invisible passing.
I asked for strong drink in the town of Strabane,
I found nourishment in the port of Derry,
A boy let me sleep chastely beside him
In a lodging house, saying I was his uncle,
A priest returned from the foreign missions.
I paid him my Irish money next morning.

Penniless, I hit the streets of Buncrana.
I warmed myself near a blacksmith's fire.
Maybe I washed myself at that same fire
For I was clean as the smith's white beard,
As the white hair that crowned his face.
He battered a shoe and the horse was patient.
The horse was a Protestant, it bowed to me,
I took a Bible out of my pocket and read
The secrets of Jesus Christ crucified.
He took pity and let me sleep in the forge.

Next morning his wife gave me porridge and eggs.
I ate with a hunger I'd never known.
Perhaps with a sorrow I had never known.
I wanted a cigarette after the meal, but
Courtesy prevented me asking, so instead
I looked into her face and thanked her
For lips, for eyes, for nose beautifully set
In the landscape of time. A Dutch word,
Landscape, I said it again and again
Till she turned and walked away. Walked through a backyard

Of a house in Holland, of a house in Donegal
Where the backdoor smelt of chickens and herrings,
Raw herring, raw flesh and fowl, a meal
For the large and loving family, brothers,
Sisters, not like my own. I sang a hymn,
I sang of God's mercy, of horses and sheep,
The creatures of God, He who's protected me
Through life's navigation, who led me to Donegal.
I heard them listening through a window
And my heart was light as a horse's shoe.

I set sail by foot the next morning,
Sure now I could find my bearings, for I was
A sailor and could walk on the water
And the streets of Buncrana were flooded with joy.
I sang the praises of the town clock that chimed,
The Protestant Church and the Catholic Chapel,
I roared with love at the purple Fahan Hill,
I bathed my feet in the lake of shadows,
And shadow I was in the sun of this town,
A foreigner seeking solace from exile.

Why was I in exile? Far from the flat lands? I climbed
Carn Mountain and I was alone. Sight I resisted
But smell led me here, the smell of yellow,
The yellow of whin, Jesus of the gorse,
The sharp Messiah, Saviour of Maoinseach Lough,
Where stories are told of water frozen
And boys and girls skating, like Holland, like home.
Then the ice broke and one was lost.
I embrace this lost boy as my child, I search
Carn Mountain for the lost bones.

They are not lost, they're in my flesh and bones.
They are purple as heather is purple.
They are flesh as flesh is drowning.
I have lost track of loneliness in Donegal.
I am growing tired of feeling at home there.
I must find a ship and head for the south.
I have a shooting star for a mouth.
When I open it, it speaks of the dead.
Its teeth are yellow and blue and red.
They chew tobacco and spit at the sky.

Still I've known peace on this mountain called Carn.
I'll take the cloth and do no one no harm.
Christ, be my guide through this difficult life.
I will weep at stone and make rock my wife.
But if my red hair were to breed with rock,
Have a child that is silence and dead and mocked,
Who would care what was revealed on this mountain?
Who would care who has paid the price of pain?
I'm leaving this place without sign or trace.
I can be lonely in another place,
Should God choose to call me. I doubt it myself.
He preferred Vermeer, the Catholic from Delft.

The Etruscan Vase

for Philip Tilling

We met their red-haired chieftain. He explained.
His people had settled in this domain
Before the moon appeared in the sacred sky,
And they believed it to be the sky's offspring,
Although the moon had given birth to itself.
Such was the innocence of this people,
An ignorance that did amuse us first,
Until he bestowed us with several gifts.

These gifts, let me describe them, Master.
A vase so deep you could sail in it,
Figured with men the shape of our gods,
And a bowl, an excellent circle,
The like of which was not filled with blood,
But instead was the blue of their eyes,
And their eyes, their Etruscan eyes, looked down
On our swords and found them wanting.

Centuries ago they'd renounced that fashion,
Turning gold instead into mirrors and leaves:
Their earth was a place for departing —
A vase, a bowl the moon had created.
And men and women, creatures of the moon,
Were fragile shadows thrown by darkness.
When it disappeared, so did they,
And death was a step in the right direction.

We listened politely. We fed them red wine.
Their blue eyes turned red as their hair.
I'd say they went out of their skulls, Master.
We skinned and boned them, used the same skulls

As bowls and vases, for the divine service,
And our swords were the fashion of fire.
We were their killers, as you required.
Their ashes we stored in the Etruscan vase.

OHIO UNIVERSITY LIBRARY
Please return this book as soon as you have finished with it. In order to avoid a fine it must be returned by the latest date stamped below. All books are subject to recall after two weeks or immediately if needed for reserve.

CF